D1468225

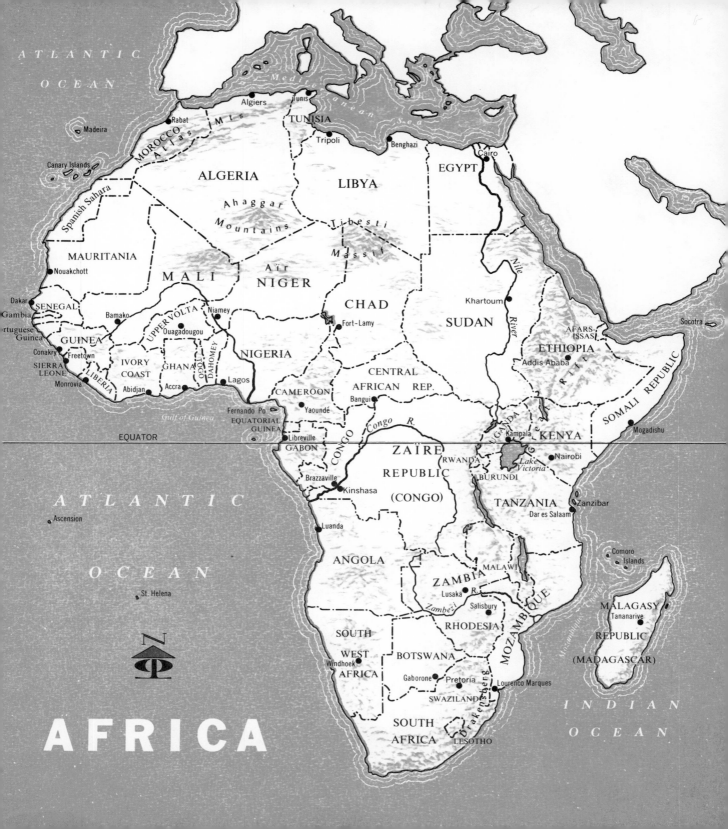

Enchantment of Africa

TANZANIA

by ALLAN CARPENTER
and JAMES W. HUGHES

Consulting Editor
John Rowe, Ph.D.
African Studies Faculty
Northwestern University
Evanston, Illinois

 CHILDRENS PRESS, CHICAGO

THE ENCHANTMENT OF AFRICA

Available now: Botswana, Burundi, Egypt, Kenya, Liberia, Malagasy Republic (Madagascar), Rwanda, Tanzania, Tunisia, Uganda, Zaire Republic (Congo Kinshasha), Zambia

Planned for the future: Algeria, Cameroon, Central African Republic, Chad, Congo (Brazzaville), Dahomey, Equatorial Guinea, Ethiopia, Gambia, Gabon, Ghana, Guinea, Ivory Coast, Lesotho, Libya, Malawi, Mali, Mauritania, Morocco, Niger, Nigeria, Rhodesia, Senegal, Sierra Leone, Somali Republic, South Africa, Sudan, Swaziland, Togo, Upper Volta

ACKNOWLEDGMENTS

Embassy of the United States of America, Dar es Salaam; Ministry of Information and Broadcasting, Dar es Salaam; Embassy of the United Republic of Tanzania, Washington, D.C.; Permanent Mission of the United Republic of Tanzania to the United Nations, New York, New York; Melville J. Herskovits Library of African Studies, Northwestern University, Evanston, Illinois.

Cover Photograph: Masai dung hut in Ngorongoro Crater, Chandler Forman
Frontispiece: Young Masai cattle herders, Tanzania Information Services

Series Coordinator: Michael Roberts
Project Editor: Joan Downing
Assistant Editor: Janis Fortman
Manuscript Editor: Elizabeth Rhein
Map Artist: Donald G. Bouma

LIBRARY OF CONGRESS
CATALOGING IN PUBLICATION DATA

Carpenter, John Allan, 1917-
    Tanzania.
    (Enchantment of Africa)

    SUMMARY: Introduces the geography, history, people, government, resources, culture, and major cities of the country boasting the highest and lowest geographic points in all Africa.
    1. Tanzania—Juvenile literature.   [1. Tanzania]
I. Hughes, James. 1934-   joint author.   II. Title.
DT438.C37   1974   916.78'03   73-20195
ISBN 0-516-04588-1

Contents

A TRUE STORY TO SET THE SCENE 7
    The Search at Olduvai Gorge

THE FACE OF THE LAND 9
    Unusual Borders—The Land Itself—High and Low—Climate

FOUR CHILDREN OF TANZANIA 17
    Ali of Kizimkazi—Sima of Tabora—Ngongo of Ngorongoro Crater—
    Julius of Moshi

TANZANIA YESTERDAY 28
    Cradle of Civilization?—The Arab Traders—The Slave Trade—
    The Slave Trade Ends—A German Colony—Rebellions—
    The Maji Maji Rebellion—World War I

TANZANIA TODAY 41
    A Strong Leader—Independent Zanzibar—Unity and Ujamaa—
    Tanzania and the World—The Government—Education

NATURAL TREASURES 57
    Mineral Treasures—Living Things

THE PEOPLE LIVE IN TANZANIA 61
    Many Differences—Fashion—The Arts—Social Problems—
    Housing—A United Country

THE PEOPLE WORK IN TANZANIA 75
    Agriculture—Business—Finance—Transportation

ENCHANTMENT OF TANZANIA 86
    Enchantment of Tanzania—Game Parks—Haven of Peace—
    High Point of Africa—Zanzibar

HANDY REFERENCE SECTION 92
    Instant Facts—Population—You Have a Date With History

INDEX 94

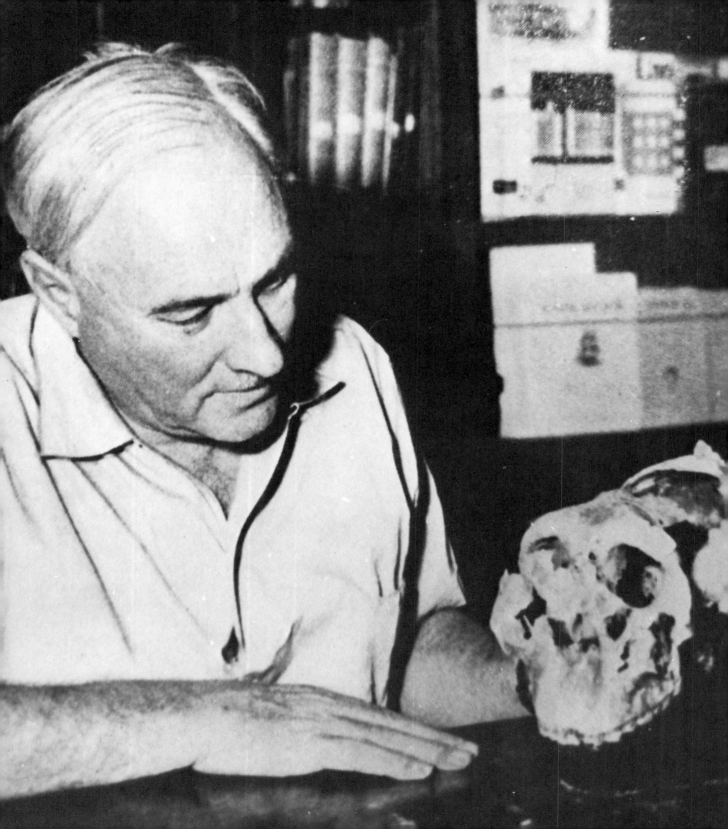

A True Story to Set the Scene

THE SEARCH AT OLDUVAI GORGE

Archaeologists, people who study the history of human life, have become interested in the African nations for a variety of reasons. Many of them believe that human life originated in Africa. A very famous archaeologist, Dr. Louis B. Leakey became fascinated with the area of northwest Tanzania because of a fossil bone he saw in a German museum in 1931. His interest in that bone led to a lifetime search in Tanzania for possible new clues to the secret of man's early existence on earth.

The fossil bone that first brought Dr. Leakey to Tanzania was found in 1911 at Olduvai Gorge, a deep canyonlike formation made by the Olduvai River. A German who collected butterflies had gone to Tanzania to study some particularly interesting species. During his travels, he stumbled on a number of fossil specimens in the sloping hills of the gorge and had taken them back to Germany at the end of his butterfly-collecting expedition. Several archaeologists became interested in these fossils because one of the bones turned out to be from a three-toed horse, long since extinct. In 1913, an expedition was sent to Olduvai Gorge for

The late archaeologist, Dr. Louis S. B. Leakey, with the skull of Zinjanthropus man. The fossilized bones of this earliest known near-human being were discovered at Olduvai Gorge, in Tanzania.

1958 ANNUAL GOVERNMENT REPORT

further study. Though many small bits of fossil material that were discovered indicated that early man could have existed in this remote region, none of the discoveries were significant enough to support such a belief.

Years later in Germany, Dr. Leakey saw this fossil collection. He had long been intrigued with the idea that man might possibly have lived in East Africa earlier than anywhere else in the world, and had already made excavations in Kenya. Because proving this theory had become Dr. Leakey's life work, he and his family set off for Tanzania to continue their search at Olduvai Gorge.

The Leakeys were at the gorge searching for fossils as often as time and money allowed. For more than twenty-five years they searched the area but unearthed nothing significant. Despite the long string of disappointments, and occasional criticisms from other archaeologists, they continued to search.

One day in May of 1959, Dr. Leakey was not feeling well. He stayed in bed at the campsite, not far from Olduvai Gorge. Mrs. Leakey, however, decided to spend a little time digging. Stopping for a moment on the steep slope of the gorge, her foot slipped out from under her and she fell against the wall of the gorge. As she fell, her hand pushed into the loose earth to grasp for support, and several chunks of soil fell away. Regaining her balance, she noticed that part of a jawbone had been exposed in the loosened clay of the gorge wall. At first she couldn't believe her eyes. She stared at the bone fragment in shocked surprise! Could this be the evidence that they had been searching for all these years? Mrs. Leakey ran back to camp, yelling, "I've found him! I've found him!"

The Leakeys named this early primate *Zinjanthropus*. Though it is not a direct ancestor of man, it is a relative of *Homo habilis* (early man). The skull bones of *Zinjanthropus* are believed to be at least 1.5 million years old. When Mrs. Leakey's discovery became known, archaeologists around the world became extremely interested in Tanzania. *Zinjanthropus* was the oldest near-human yet discovered. The Leakeys had spent a lifetime of searching in Tanzania to prove their theory that East Africa was the origin of mankind. For many other people, however, *Zinjanthropus* became yet another reason for learning more about Tanzania, one of the most fascinating East African nations.

The Face of the Land

Tanzania is bordered by eight nations and one ocean, the Indian Ocean, which makes up the entire eastern border of Tanzania. Part of the country is even located *in* the ocean—a group of three islands that have been given the collective name of Zanzibar. The beautiful Indian Ocean supplies Tanzania with many excellent

outlets to the world through its ports, and also provides fine beaches and seaside resorts enjoyed by people from all over the world.

Though the eastern border of Tanzania is on the Indian Ocean, the country is surrounded by land on the north, south, and west. The eight nations bordering Tanzania include Kenya and Uganda, which together with Tanzania are often called East Africa. These countries form the northern and northeastern borders. South of Tanzania are Zambia, Malawi, and Mozambique (a Portuguese colony). On the west are Rwanda, Burundi, and Zaïre. (Until 1971, Zaïre was called The Democratic Republic of the Congo.)

Unlike most African countries, many of Tanzania's inland borders have large bodies of water: Tanzania's borders with Malawi, Mozambique, Rwanda, and Burundi run through the largest lakes in Africa. In the west, the border passes through lakes Victoria and Tanganyika,

major waterways within East Africa. The border shared with Malawi and Mozambique passes through Lake Malawi.

These enormous lakes are part of the great Rift Valley, which extends all the way from Jordan in the Middle East to south-central Africa. The Rift Valley is caused by a *fault,* a weak place in the earth. Terrain along the path of the Rift Valley is constantly changing, as it has been for millions of years. New mountains are being formed, lakes are drying up to become deserts, and flatland is becoming hilly. These changes take place very slowly. It might take thousands of years for a lake to become a desert. Someday, perhaps, the lakes that surround Tanzania might even be gone.

THE LAND ITSELF

The mainland area of Tanzania occupies 363,708 square miles of land. The

MAP KEY

Arusha, B4	Kibondo, B1	Lindi, E6	Mpanda, D1	Rufiji River, D5
Babati, C4	Kigoma, C1	Liwale, E5	Mtalika, F4	Rungwa, D3
Bagamoyo, D5	Kilombero River, E4	Luguruka, E4	Mtwara, E6	Rungwa River, D2
Biharamulo, B2	Kilosa, D4	Luwegu River, E4	Mufindi, E4	Ruvuma River, F5
Bukoba, A2	Kilwa Kivinji, E6	Mafia Channel, D6	Muhinji Chini, E5	Same, B5
Bunazi, A2	Kimambi, E5	Mafia Island, D6	Musoma, A3	Serengeti
Central Plateau, D2	Kipengere Range, E3	Mahenge, E4	Mvomero, D5	National Park, B3
Chunya, E3	Kipili, D.	Makumbako, E3	Mwanza, B2	Shinyanga, B3
Dar es Salaam, D5	Kisarawe, D5	Malagarasi River, C1	Mwaya, E3	Simiyu River, B3
Dodoma, D4	Kitunda, D2	Manda, E3	Naakanazi, B1	Singida, C3
Geita, B2	Kizimkazi, D5	Manyoni, C3	Nachingwea, E5	Songea, F4
Great Ruaha River, D4	Kondoa, C4	Masai Steppe, C4	Newala, F5	Sumbawanga, D2
Handeni, C5	Kongwa, D4	Masasi, F5	Ngara, B1	Tabora, C2
Hogoro, C4	Korogwe, C5	Mbamba Bay, F3	Ngorongoro	Tanga, C5
Ifakara, D4	Lake Egasi, B3	Mbeya, E3	Crater, B3	Tunduma, E2
Ifunda, D4	Lake Manyara, B4	Mbwemburu River, E5	Njinjo, E5	Tunduru, F4
Ikola, D1	Lake Manyara	Mchinga, E6	Njombe, E3	Ugalla River, C2
Ipole, C2	National Park, B4	Mikumi	Njombe River, D3	Ujiji, C1
Iringa, D4	Lake Natron, B4	National Park, D4	Nkonko, D3	Urambo, C2
Itigi, C3	Lake Nyasa	Mkata, C5	Nzega, C2	Utete, D5
Ivuna, D2	(Lake Malawi), F3	Mkokotoni, C5	Olduvai Gorge, B4	Uvinza, C1
Kagera River, A1	Lake Rukwa, D2	Morogoro, D5	Pangani River, C5	Wami River, D5
Kahama, B2	Lake	Moshi, B4	Pemba Channel, C6	Wete, C6
Kaliua, C2	Tanganyika, C1, D1	Mount	Pemba Island, C6	Zanzibar, C5
Kufufu River, D2	Lake Victoria, A2	Kilimanjaro, B4	Ruaha	Zanzibar Channel, C5
Kibiti, D5	Liganga, E3	Moyowosi River, B2	National Park, D3	Zanzibar Island, C5

island area, comprised of three islands—Zanzibar, Pemba, and Mafia—has a combined area of 1,020 square miles. Tanzania's land area is twice as great as either of its East African neighbors, Kenya and Uganda.

Along the Indian Ocean, the mainland is low in elevation and is tropical in climate and vegetation. Farther inland, the land rises abruptly to a plateau region which extends through East Africa. It is cut deeply by the great Rift Valley and broken into two faults: the eastern rift and the western rift. About forty miles inland the eastern plateau begins; it rises to about two thousand feet above sea level. This plateau is broken by the eastern rift.

Beyond it is the central plateau, with an elevation averaging four thousand feet and rising in many areas to as much as six thousand feet.

Much of the central plateau area is dry grassland called *savanna,* not at all suited for farming. These vast plains have instead been used by nomadic cattle herders for centuries. These people moved their cattle across and beyond the central plateau in constant search of fresh grazing lands and water. The country's enormous wildlife populations also live on the savanna. Serengeti National Park is one of the largest wildlife sanctuaries in the world, currently protecting thousands of animals. Fertile areas good for farming are

African fisherwomen drag their nets for small fish at Lindi, on the Indian Ocean.

found in the higher, hilly regions of south-west and northeast Tanzania, as well as along the shorelines of lakes Victoria and Tanganyika.

West of the central plateau is the western fault of the great Rift Valley. This includes lakes Tanganyika and Malawi, and passes through the western border of Tanzania.

HIGH AND LOW

Tanzania's most famous feature is probably Mount Kilimanjaro. This extinct volcano is the highest mountain peak in the entire African continent, rising 19,391 feet above sea level. The top of the mountain is very unusual; twin peaks are separated by a flat saddle area more than seven miles wide at the top. From a distance, the mountain's shape resembles a huge stool or chair.

Tanzania not only has the highest point of all Africa within its borders, but it can boast of having the lowest point as well. It is believed that the lowest elevation in Africa is to be found at the bottom of Lake Tanganyika, which has been measured to be two thousand feet below sea level. This lake's extreme depth is believed to have been caused by the same pressures inside the earth that created the entire Rift Valley.

Two Chagga women on the slopes of Mount Kilimanjaro, the highest mountain in Africa.

CLIMATE

Tanzania's climate is influenced by many factors: the country's nearness to the equator, the number of large bodies of water surrounding the land, and the elevation of the land.

Along the flat coastal regions the climate is usually hot and humid, though at times the ocean breezes cool things off. Here temperatures vary between eighty and ninety degrees Fahrenheit. In the central plateau area, with a higher elevation, the weather is often quite warm and dry. The climate becomes cooler and milder, however, in the border regions where the land is hilly and mountainous, and where many huge lakes are found. Occasional frosts have even been experienced here.

There is no summer, fall, winter, or spring in Tanzania, as in the temperate climates of the United States and Europe. This is because Tanzania is so close to the equator. Seasons here are divided into two categories, dry and rainy. Southern Tanzania has one big rainy season—from November to April. In the northern part of the country, the rainy season usually comes twice each year. The "short rains" occur during October or November and last only about a month. During these times, rain falls heavily for brief moments either in the early morning, at noon, or again in the evening. The "long rains" start around March, often extending into early June. Much more rain falls during these times than during the season of short rains. Because the rest of the year usually shows little rain, it is usually referred to as the "dry season." Along the Indian Ocean coast the annual rainfall is approximately fifty to sixty inches. The central plateau averages less than thirty inches and the southwestern, northeastern, and shoreline highland accumulation varies from forty to one hundred inches in a year.

Southwestern mountain range near Iringa.

15

Four Children of Tanzania

ALI OF KIZIMKAZI

Ali lives with his parents and two sisters in Kizimkazi on the island of Zanzibar. Ali is eleven years old, the youngest child in his family. His father and several of their neighbors work on a small plot of land nearby on which many coconut palms grow. The plot of land was given to the families for a cooperative farm after Zanzibar became part of independent Tanzania in 1964. Each family that works on a particular plot of land owns a share in the land and keeps its share of the crops. Almost all the people in Ali's village work on some kind of cooperative farm.

Ali helps his father with the work at the cooperative coconut grove by climbing the tall, thin palms and loosening the coconuts so they drop to the ground below.

Ali's home is similar to the houses in Kizimkazi. The basic structure of the house is made by packing mud and pieces of coral into the framework. The exterior is then whitewashed to make the home

look neat and clean. The white walls also help reflect the hot rays of the sun, keeping the inside cool and comfortable. Inside the house is a main sitting room where the family and their friends spend most of their time. To the rear of the house are several small sleeping rooms. Ali's mother and sisters do much of the cooking on outside fireplaces or in cooking pots in the courtyard that surrounds the rear of the house. This courtyard also has space for a patch of banana trees and a small vegetable garden. Ali's mother and sisters take care of the cooking and gardening chores while the men work in their coconut grove.

Ali and his family are followers of Islam. On Friday, the most important religious day of the week for Moslems, Ali and his father wear the Moslem *kanzu* (a long, white shirt or robe similar to a Roman toga) and cap when they go to the mosque (place of worship) to pray. This type of dress is also worn on holidays.

Since the climate in Zanzibar is usually rather warm, Ali wears only a pair of khaki shorts when he is not at school. Although Ali and most of his friends wear short-sleeved shirts to school, they prefer not to wear shirts during the heat of the day. At home, Ali's mother and sisters wear traditional wraparound dresses made of kanga cloth. When they go to the public market or to the city, however, they cover themselves with a black *bui bui,* which is a traditional Moslem outfit. It is worn over the normal dress and allows a woman to shield her body and face from direct view. Most traditional Moslem women in Zanzibar do not like to expose their faces to strangers.

Ali's father wears khaki shorts most of the time while he is working. Once the day's work is finished, however, Ali's father wraps his *kikoi,* a checkered waist cloth, over the shorts, as is the custom in the coastal regions.

Since Ali is a strong, capable boy, his father expects him to help with the work at the coconut grove. Ali is able to climb rapidly to the top of the tall, thin coconut palms. At the top, he loosens the coconuts so they drop to the ground below. Then the men in the cooperative gather the coconuts and haul the heavy loads of coconuts to the main shed.

There some workers remove the thick husks that encase the coconut, while others open and split the coconut. As this is done, the coconut milk is collected. The milk is sold in the market for a variety of purposes. It makes a refreshing cool drink that is very popular with the local people. It is also used for cooking. The most important part of the coconut is the white meat, called *copra*. The men dry this meat in hot ovens and then sell it. Copra is exported to markets all over the world.

Ali's family earns enough money from the coconut cooperative to maintain their home and to feed and clothe everyone. The small vegetable and fruit garden maintained by Ali's mother also helps keep expenses to a minimum. There is rarely any extra money for savings, but Ali's father does not mind. He remembers the days when most families had little or nothing and were forced to work almost like slaves. That was during the days when a rich sultan and a small number of rich landowners controlled most of Zanzibar.

Ali has been able to attend primary school and is in Standard 6 (sixth grade). He enjoys schoolwork and does fairly well with his subjects, but he will probably not go beyond Standard 7. His family cannot afford to send him to one of the secondary schools. Besides, Ali is needed on the cooperative to help his father. Perhaps Ali can continue his education by taking correspondence classes through the mail after he has saved some money.

MICHAEL ROBERTS

JAMES HUGHES

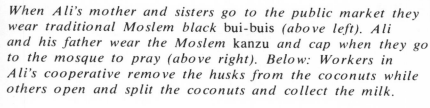

When Ali's mother and sisters go to the public market they wear traditional Moslem black bui-buis *(above left). Ali and his father wear the Moslem* kanzu *and cap when they go to the mosque to pray (above right). Below: Workers in Ali's cooperative remove the husks from the coconuts while others open and split the coconuts and collect the milk.*

TANZANIA INFORMATION SERVICES

Sima's family owns a small duka (shop) in the dry plateau region near Tabora. Their store, like the one shown above, is stocked with a variety of items needed by the customers, most of whom come from the surrounding countryside.

SIMA OF TABORA

Sima is seven years old, and the second oldest of three children in her family. Her family owns a small *duka* (shop) at one of the crossroads leading into the town of Tabora.

The building in which Sima lives is both store and home. The front portion is used as the store, while the rear portion provides enough space for the family to live. Most of the people who trade in the *duka* come from the surrounding countryside. There are not many stores in the dry plateau region, and many people have to travel far to get to one. Some of the customers are cattle herders who travel around in search of fresh grass and water for their herds. Sima enjoys listening to the stories told by these traveling people. She misses many of these friendly customers when they move on to another place, but is always excited when they return.

Sima's parents work hard to make a living for the family. Their store is stocked with such items as dried foods and spices, assorted canned foods, soap, flashlight batteries, wire, kerosene, and flour. Some fresh foods are sold when they are available. All these items are usually brought in by truck or rail from the capital city, Dar es Salaam, on the Indian Ocean coast. Since the store's stock must come such a distance, prices are much higher than in shops closer to the coast. The family tries to sell all of its stock, rather than using any themselves. Therefore, in order to feed the family, Sima's father must raise a few goats, which provide both milk and meat for the family. Sima's mother also has a small garden in which she grows some vegetables for her family. Sometimes, however, lack of rain makes her vegetables wither and dry up.

For two years, a school in Tabora was run by Protestant missionaries. Every day, Sima and her sister Mary walked the few miles to town so they could attend the school. Though the teachers were from Germany, they spoke the local language, called Ki-nyamwezi.

The music teacher had a small, portable organ. At the end of each schoolday, the children and the teachers gathered around the organ to sing. Sima was not at all bashful about her love of music. Often she sang songs of her people for everyone in the class to hear. The music teacher also taught Sima and her classmates many songs they had never heard before.

Suddenly the missionary school was closed. The German missionary group did not have enough money to keep the school open, so the teachers returned to their own country. Now Sima and Mary stay home and help out in the store.

Because Sima's parents still want Sima to have an education, they want to send her to live with an aunt in the city of Arusha so she can go to school there. Arusha is almost two hundred miles from Tabora. It has many fine schools, and Sima's aunt has enough room and enough money to care for Sima as well as for her own children. Sima's parents think it is important for Sima to continue with school, though they do not like the idea of sending her so far away to live for most of the year.

If Sima goes to live with her aunt, Sima's father thinks he, too, might move to Arusha and seek work in this larger, rapidly growing city. He does not want to give up the store, but he knows he could probably make more money in the city. Times are changing very fast in Tanzania, and Sima's parents are anxious for all the family to benefit from some of these changes.

NGONGO OF NGORONGORO CRATER

Ngongo knows that his life is very different from that of many other ten-year-old boys and girls: Ngongo does not live in one place all year round. Instead, he and his family travel throughout the cattle grazing lands of East Africa in search of food and water for their cattle. The family's "home" is near the Ngorongoro Crater region in Tanzania. But since they have so many cattle, which need water and fresh grasses all year long, they must constantly move their herd around the countryside in search of better grazing areas. Ngongo's people, the Masai, do not have farms where they can grow feed for the animals. They are *semi-nomadic* cattle herders; that is, they take the same route every year with their cattle. In fact, cattle enclosures and *bomas* (temporary homes) have been built along this route over the years. These bomas are usually about one day's walking distance apart. The family needs to carry only its cooking utensils and a few household and sleeping articles on these journeys.

A Masai family includes more people than just parents and children. Aunts, uncles, nephews, nieces, brothers, and sisters are also part of the immediate family. Everyone works together and lives in the same boma.

Although Ngongo has never attended school, he is very smart and knowledgeable about many things. The older men see that young boys like Ngongo learn the history and traditions of the Masai people. One tradition that Ngongo knows well is that of responsibility to one's age-mates. Boys born in the same year are considered age-mates; a person's love for and responsibility to other members of his age-group is often greater than that for members of his family.

The elders teach Masai boys many other things, too, such as how to take proper care of cattle, how to gather food, and how to hunt well. All these skills will help the boys to be useful and respected by their people. It is important that Ngongo un-

These Masai boys have been taking part in a coming-of-age ceremonial dance that is part of their induction into the warrior class.

22

derstands as much as possible about good cattle raising, since cattle are the most important thing in the life of the traditional Masai.

According to beliefs among the Masai, all cattle were placed on this earth for Masai alone. The cattle supplied them with food, as well as with material to make clothing and build shelter. The Masai had everything they needed as long as they had their cattle and the freedom to move about the land in search of fresh water and grazing lands. The many recent changes that have occurred throughout East Africa are affecting the traditional way of life for the Masai. The elders of the family in Ngongo's clan have been concerned about some of these changes.

Ngongo takes his turn tending the family cattle herd, as does this Masai boy who lives near the Ngorongoro Crater.

In earlier times, much of the land in two of the East African nations was "Masai land." But national boundaries now separate Tanzania, Uganda, and Kenya. It has become more difficult for Masai to move freely among these nations with their cattle. The governments of the East African nations have taught the Masai new methods of farming and land development. Many pieces of land are now being fenced off and restricted for private farms. The Masai are not sure what will happen to them and their cattle if people continue to take over land and restrict its use.

A representative from the Tanzanian government has talked several times with the elders of Ngongo's clan. He wants the clan to settle down in one area near Ngorongoro Crater. This man said that if the clan settled there, the government would send people there to teach them how to take care of their cattle without having to migrate every year. Of course, this means the Masai would have to farm and control the land much differently than ever before. The new government of Tanzania wants to help the Masai develop a more modern and more productive style of living. Not all of the Masai elders are convinced that such changes are necessary.

Ngongo himself has seen some of the newer clothing, cars, and radios of the city people, but he is not sure if he wants these things. He is used to the yearly travels with the cattle. He enjoys this way of life, and so does his family. What would life be like if there were no more cattle migration? Would he enjoy the new ranching life? Would there be enough water and grazing land? Ngongo wonders. Already in his short lifetime, Ngongo has witnessed many changes in East Africa. But it is not for Ngongo to decide. Right now his job is to care for the cattle. The elders of his tribe will discuss these problems and decide what is best for all.

JULIUS OF MOSHI

Julius lives in the fast-growing city of Moshi, only twenty-five miles from Africa's mightiest peak, Mount Kilimanjaro. On most days, Julius can see the mountain quite clearly from his home.

Julius has three younger brothers. This year he is twelve years old and will complete Standard 7 (seventh grade) at the end of the school year.

Julius's father is the district development officer in charge of agriculture for the area. He teaches people in his area about the new farming methods, helps them farm, as well as helping them develop cooperative ways of working. Under the new Tanzanian government's *ujamaa* program, people are asked to join together to develop the land and provide a better standard of living for everyone. To do this, they form cooperatives. Instead of each farmer working by himself to grow and market his farm products, farmers band together to work a large area of land and sell the produce. Everyone shares equally in the benefits gained from the cooperative efforts.

25

Both Julius's mother and father often travel to other villages to discuss the idea of *ujamaa* with the people. Julius and his brothers enjoy attending these meetings with their parents. Although Julius's younger brothers seem to like playing with the local children more than listening to the speeches at the meetings, Julius has begun to take an interest in the meetings. His father often comments on how important these meetings are, and Julius wants to learn as much as he can about his native land.

Julius completes Standard 7 this year; he hopes that he will qualify for admission to one of the secondary schools. Julius has always received very high grades in school and his mother and father would like him to attend the University of Dar es Salaam someday. Julius thinks he might want to be a doctor, but he has a few years yet to decide.

Julius and his family live in a modest home near one of the cooperative coffee plantations. The house has a large living room, dining room, kitchen, and several bedrooms. The four boys share one of the larger bedrooms upstairs. With his brothers in the same room, Julius often finds it difficult to concentrate on his schoolwork. His younger brothers are constantly walking in and out of the room—talking, laughing, and getting in his way. Usually Julius lets his younger brothers play in the bedroom, and he takes his schoolwork down to the dining room.

Julius is a runner on the school's track team and also captain of the football team. (Football in most of Europe and Africa is the game that Americans call soccer.) Julius enjoys sports very much and thinks he will be active in sports next year when he attends secondary school. At school, everyone also works in the cooperative garden after classes are finished for the day. Julius is glad he can share his extra knowledge about farming with his classmates in this project, and his father is happy that Julius is interested in farming.

On Independence Day, April 26, the family is planning to drive to Dar es Salaam, where Julius's grandparents live. Julius is anxious to see the large parades, fireworks, and festivals held in the capital city. The family will spend a week visiting in Dar es Salaam, and Julius's grandfather has promised to take him swimming in the ocean. They may even have a chance to fish and dive in the calmer waters south of the ocean port. If they are lucky, they may even see the president of Tanzania, President Nyerere, in person when he makes his major address to the nation on Independence Day.

Julius and his family live in the city of Moshi (opposite), only twenty-five miles away from Mount Kilimanjaro (background).

UNITED NATIONS

Tanzania Yesterday

CRADLE OF CIVILIZATION?

The three nations of East Africa have become internationally famous due to man's search for two "unknowns." In the 1800s in Uganda, explorers searched for the source of the Nile River and named Lake Victoria "the cradle of the Nile." With the recent fossil discoveries in Tanzania and Kenya, East Africa may become known to the world as "the cradle of civilization."

Olduvai Gorge in Tanzania was the first place where archaeologists discovered evidence suggesting that the earliest human beings lived in East Africa. Here fossil fragments were found of *Homo habilis,* an early man who lived 2.0 million years ago. More recently evidence has been unearthed at Lake Rudolf in nearby Kenya that dates the oldest East African human at 2.8 million years. Richard Leakey, son of the late archaeologist, Louis B. Leakey, is convinced that man originated in Africa and slowly spread to the other continents.

The mainland of Tanzania contains many secrets about the early life of human beings. It is believed that early people lived here during the Neolithic Age (sometimes called the New Stone Age). These people probably lived in small family groups and depended on agriculture for their survival. Some of the family groups may have moved about in search of better farmland, spreading out to other regions of East Africa. Initially, these individual families probably governed themselves, but as more family groups developed and lived near one another, chiefs were recognized who ruled over a number of families grouped into a village. Some of these villages grew into larger states, or kingdoms, which combined many village areas. One of the largest known early villages was called Engaruka, and was located on the slopes of the Rift Valley near Ngorongoro Crater. More than several thousand people may have lived there at one time, using irrigation to grow crops. Eventually the village was abandoned, probably when its source of water dried up. (Nomadic tribes might have come upon this large settled area and destroyed the village through a series of wars.) In parts of mainland Tanzania, many village states probably developed. Clusters of village states were ruled by tribal chieftains and kings, especially in the region west of Lake Victoria, where a number of kingdoms have existed since about A.D. 1500. Later, other states were founded in the highlands around Mount Kilimanjaro.

There were also many villages on the island of Zanzibar and near the coast of the mainland. As early as A.D. 700, settlements were known to exist on the island of Zanzibar, then called Uguja by the local people. Simple huts made of clay and plastered on a framework of poles stuck into the ground were typical of the homes constructed on the islands and near the coastal areas.

Pottery fragments that originally came from Persia (now Iran) have been found in the coastal area. This indicates that people from other parts of the world visited Tanzania in very early times.

THE ARAB TRADERS

The Islamic religion was probably brought to the islands of Pemba and Zanzibar about the year 900. The early Arabs who came to this region named the whole area, including the largest island. They called it *Zanzibar,* which means in Arabic "the coastland of the Africans." These Arabs soon brought their religion and way of life to East Africa, marking the beginning of the Swahili culture. Swahili refers to the combination of the two cultures, African and Arab.

The Arab people settled on the offshore islands, as well as in many of the coastal mainland towns. With the African people, they developed many trading cities and seaport towns. As the Arabs settled and intermarried with the Africans, they also converted many to their religion—Islam. A stone mosque built in this area about 1100 A.D. is still being used as a place of worship.

By the beginning of the fourteenth century, the Arabs were well settled in East Africa, and the region's assets were becoming well known in the Arab world. In 1331, when the Arab explorer Ibn Battuta visited the seaport town of Kilwa on the Tanzanian coast, he reported, "Kilwa is a most beautiful and well-constructed town."

About this time a great palace called "Husuni Kubwa" was built at Kilwa. It contained courtyards, an octagonal swimming pool, vaulted and domed ceilings, many sleeping rooms, and carved decorations and niches for oil lamps. Nearby was a huge royal warehouse with thirty-nine storage rooms. The king minted his own coins and managed to dominate the trade of the whole coast, especially the gold trade from the Sofala area of Mozambique to the south.

When the Arabs first arrived they concentrated their energies in developing the island and coastal regions of Tanzania, establishing lush clove plantations on Zanzibar. The Arabs soon found that they needed labor to operate the clove plantations; they also became interested in the ivory trade of the East African interior.

Gradually, in the nineteenth century, Arab traders pushed into the interior of East Africa, establishing trading centers. Trade routes were established from the coast inland to Tabora and other settlements. A trip from the interior to the mainland was extremely slow and difficult, but the demand for ivory and cheap labor was great.

The Arabs began to take slaves from some of the interior villages to transport the heavy ivory to the coast. Soon slaves as well as ivory became an important part of the economic life of the Arab traders. In southern Tanzania the early trading routes were "slaving routes." Slave markets sprang up at Zanzibar and Kilwa. The unfortunate slaves were shipped from there to many parts of the Middle East.

THE SLAVE TRADE

The slave trade is one of the oldest and cruelest forms of human abuse. In many areas of the world, including parts of Africa, it had been common practice to use prisoners of war as household slaves following a battle. When the demand grew in the nineteenth century for slaves to work on clove and sugar plantations, Arab traders in the interior encouraged people to sell or trade slaves with them. They also

Site of the slave auction center on Zanzibar.

encouraged rival groups to raid each other's villages for the purpose of stealing slaves. When the Arab traders introduced guns and gunpowder to the Africans, large numbers of slaves could be captured by a small number of raiders. The slave trade flourished; thousands of people were taken from their villages and forced to walk hundreds of miles to the seacoast.

As few as six leaders and fifty helpers with guns were able to gather more than one thousand slaves at a time. This small band would surround a village; when least suspected, they would rush in and set fire to the area. Others from the raiding party would capture as many people as possible, killing off the old and wounded and leaving the village a burned ruin. Once captured, the slaves were chained around their necks with their hands bound behind their backs. Two slaves were then held together by a yoke in the shape of a forked bar, and forced to carry heavy loads of ivory by resting them on their heads and shoulders. Often slaves who became too weak for the burden or the long trip were killed along the way so they would not slow down the progress to the slave market. For every slave who reached the coast alive, five slaves may have died along the way.

The main slave routes in East Africa were located in southern Tanzania. The interior routes north of modern Tanzania were controlled by the Masai. Because these people were unfriendly to the foreigners, the slave routes stayed to the south. Also, in northern Tanzania were powerful kingdoms strong enough to protect themselves from slaving attacks.

In those days, a trip from the interior of Tanzania to the coast might have taken as long as two years to complete. The town of Tabora in the interior became infamous as a gathering point for the trade of ivory. Slaves from the Congo were also occasionally transported through Tabora to the coast. Zanzibar and Kilwa on the coast were disgraced by their slave markets. No one knows the exact number of slaves that were actually taken from East Africa, but it is estimated that thousands of slaves were sent to the Middle East; some were even sent to European colonies in southern Africa, South America, and North America.

Explorers from Europe began to visit the coast of East Africa during the sixteenth century, partly to seek a shorter, eastern route to India. Until that time, ships had to travel all the way down the coast of Africa, around the Cape of Good Hope, and back up through the Indian Ocean. Portugal sent several expeditions to find a shortcut to India. Vasco da Gama, one of the most famous Portuguese explorers, arrived near the East African coast as early as 1502, and other expeditions landed at the town of Kilwa in 1505. The Portuguese and Arabs engaged in conflicts over these territories as time wore on, since the Portuguese tried to take control of the coastal ports and enforce a monopoly over sea trade.

Later, the Dutch, Germans, English, and Americans sent trade embassies to this

Arabs came to the islands of Pemba and Zanzibar as early as the year 900, bringing the Islamic religion with them. The mosque below was built at Kilwa in the twelfth century. The Portuguese, who arrived in the sixteenth century, fought with the Arabs over these territories. During the conflicts, the Portuguese built forts at Chake Chake, Pemba (opposite) and Kilwa (above).

part of the world. They were eager to trade manufactured cloth and other goods for East African ivory.

THE SLAVE TRADE ENDS

As the slave trade prospered in Zanzibar, the Sultan of Zanzibar continued to encourage greater markets with the Europeans in such items as cloves, cinnamon, and copra (dried coconut meat from which coconut oil is extracted). He also built up the ivory and slave markets.

Especially in Britain, people were very much against the idea of slavery and some religious groups protested violently. One of the leaders of this protest movement was the missionary-explorer, Dr. David Livingstone, who traveled extensively in eastern and central Africa during the 1860s and 1870s.

Reports of Dr. Livingstone's explorations were published in leading newspapers all over the world. In letters describing his travels, he told of the great injustices brought on by the slave trade. He appealed to his readers to encourage the end of the slave trade. His writings aroused a great deal of sympathy and concern for the African people.

Suddenly Livingstone's letters home ceased. Fear arose that he was lost or killed. Henry Morton Stanley, then a reporter for a New York City newspaper, went to Africa to look for Livingstone. In November of 1871, Stanley entered the town of Ujiji, on Lake Tanganyika. Upon seeing an aged European man in the midst of the Africans, he extended a hand of friendship. Not knowing what to say, he uttered what was to become a classic phrase: "Dr. Livingstone, I presume?"

Dr. Livingstone had not been lost. He had just been busy with his missionary hospital work, and had failed to keep up with his correspondence to Europe. Livingstone and Stanley traveled together for a few months; then Stanley continued his own exploration in Africa. Livingstone went back to Ujiji and into the Congo, hoping to reach Katanga province. Livingstone died in the Congo in 1873. His loyal African friends wrapped his body in sailcloth and carried the remains six hundred miles to the coast. From there, the body was shipped home to England for final burial in Westminster Abbey, which has been the burial place of notable Englishmen for hundreds of years.

Dr. Livingstone and others had helped alert the conscience of the world to the great injustices of slavery. By the 1870s the British had forced the Sultan of Zanzibar to restrict and finally eliminate the slave trade.

This monument at Ujiji marks the spot where Henry Morton Stanley first met Dr. David Livingstone.

TANGANYIKA NEWS REVIEW

On the island of Zanzibar today is the Cathedral Church of Christ. It was built on the exact spot where the slave auctions were once held. The altar of the church is situated on the spot where the slaves were whipped as a form of punishment.

A GERMAN COLONY

East Africa had become the focus of great international attention. The Germans and Belgians, as well as the British, had become interested in the potential of this region and sent explorers into East Africa to establish possible claims for colonial territories. Because European nations were rivaling each other for control of various parts of Africa, a conference was held in Berlin, Germany in 1884-85 to discuss the problem. At this conference the major European powers divided the African continent into coastal "spheres of interest." No other European nation would be allowed to interfere in a particular nation's sphere of interest, and it was the responsibility of each nation to develop its area. A race to claim interior territories ensued, which brought European domination to all of Africa by the beginning of the twentieth century.

As a result of explorations into areas of Tanganyika (the old name for mainland Tanzania) by Karl Peters in 1884, Germany was granted control over this area. Britain, however, had acquired control over the island of Zanzibar, as well as the neighboring territories of Kenya and Uganda. Both Britain and Germany fought wars of conquest against Africans before they were able to make good their claims. These wars were termed "punitive expeditions." Though many Africans bravely resisted, they were unable to overcome European superiority with machine guns and cannon.

The Germans hoped to gain great wealth from their African colony. They knew that the land had good agricultural potential, and German farmers were sent to Tanganyika to start plantations of coffee, tobacco, and sisal (a plant that produces a twinelike white fiber). The Germans knew these crops would sell easily on the world market and bring in a certain amount of cash. In order to make the greatest possible profit from these farms, the German colonialists forced Africans to work on the plantations without pay. They also claimed all the land that was not already being used by Africans. Africans were forced to pay taxes to the German government for the services and protection of the colonial government.

The German government appointed Karl Peters ruler of the district around

The Cathedral Church of Christ (opposite) is built on the exact spot where slave auctions were held on Zanzibar.

JAMES HUGHES

Mount Kilimanjaro. He was extremely harsh and cruel to the African people. In fact, his reputation was so bad that the local people called him *Mkono Wa Damu* or "the man with blood on his hands." The forced labor, taxes, and cruel treatment were deeply resented by the local people.

REBELLIONS

Mkwawa, chief of the Hehe people in the southern highlands of Tanganyika, was very much against the invasion of his land by the Germans. He knew that African weapons were no match against those of the Germans. In spite of this, his people decided to fight against the European invaders. Mkwawa and his men wiped out the first German troops sent to occupy their lands. Three years went by before the Germans managed to capture Mkwawa's capital at Iringa in 1893. Mkwawa escaped but had to remain in hiding. The Germans tried to hunt him down. For several years, Mkwawa was able to avoid German capture because his people continued to be loyal to him. In June of 1898, however, he was trapped. Rather than be taken prisoner, Mkwawa shot himself. His resistance to the colonial rule is still well remembered by his people, and his braveness and courage make him a hero to African people everywhere.

THE MAJI
MAJI REBELLION

German colonial rule continued to be harsh and severe toward the African people. When the colonial government required the Africans to cultivate cotton for export without receiving anything in return, the people in southern Tanganyika again rebelled. This armed resistance started in 1905 near Kilwa. People took an oath to fight as long as necessary to get rid of the German intruders. Medicine men sprinkled the fighters with a compound called *maji,* made of water, millet, and maize. The maji, which gave the rebellion its name, was believed to have magic powers that would turn German bullets into water.

The rebellion spread all across southern Tanzania and lasted more than a year. Eventually the modern weapons of the Germans slaughtered many of the rebelling Africans, and the Germans took brutal reprisals on African villages. Farmlands of the rebelling peoples were set afire and destroyed, creating extreme fam-

In the late nineteenth and early twentieth century, the German colonial government forced the Africans to cultivate cotton for export without receiving anything in return. The Africans resisted this harsh rule in what became known as the Maji Maji Rebellion.

ine in the region. More than 120,000 Africans were killed from either fighting or famine during the Maji Maji Rebellion.

WORLD WAR I

During World War I, colonial forces of the Germans and British fought against one another in East Africa, much as their home forces were doing in Europe. The Germans had hoped to disrupt the Kenya railway, which was providing vast amounts of food to the Allied armies. The British wanted to blockade the port of Dar es Salaam, used by the German navy. With the assistance of South African troops and Belgian soldiers, the British prevented German troops from entering Kenya. They also sank a German cruiser, the *Koenigsburg,* in the delta of the Rufiji River of Tanganyika, thus blocking the German port. This was the first time airplanes were used in an East African battle.

World War I ended in 1918; in 1919 Germany was forced by the newly formed League of Nations to give up its Tanganyikan claims to the British. Now all of East Africa—Zanzibar, Tanganyika, Kenya, and Uganda—came under the colonial rule of Britain. British rule was milder than German rule had been but the African population preferred independence to even the mildest form of foreign rule. When British colonial rule began in the territory of Tanganyika, Tanganyikan Africans were already taking steps to protect their rights and interests.

Tanzania Today

Tanganyika and Zanzibar were to be under British rule for almost fifty years before independence was finally granted. As time went on, the local people began to be more vocal in their desire to be free of alien controls. Even before the British came to power, Mkwawa's resistance and the Maji Maji rebellion showed that the local people resented interference by foreign powers. An Arab Sultan ruled Zanzibar under British protection, and a British colonial governor ruled on the mainland of Tanganyika.

To achieve their goal of independence, the African people had to band together. As early as 1922, the Tanganyika Territory African Civil Servants Association was formed as a social club for Africans employed by the government. The members discussed many issues related to their welfare and progress. Later, the name of this organization was changed to the Tanganyika African Association so it could include all Africans. By 1954 this association was a well-organized and powerful force in the territory. Once again its name was changed, this time to Tanganyikan African National Union (TANU). The organization then became a powerful political party whose main aim was independence for the territory.

In 1946, after World War II, the new United Nations (UN) took responsibility for Tanganyika. Though the territory became a UN Trusteeship, Britain stayed on as the administrator. This situation stayed in effect until independence in 1961.

A STRONG LEADER

Julius Nyerere entered Tanganyikan politics in the early 1950s. He had received his Diploma in Education from

December 9, 1961, was Independence Day in Tanganyika. At the airport, two African chiefs (left) wait for H.R.H. Prince Philip to arrive for the ceremonies. Below: Children wave flags along the streets as they wait for Prince Philip to pass by.

Makerere College in Uganda and had gone to Edinburgh University in Scotland for his Master of Arts degree. This education gave him the qualifications necessary to rise to the top of the civil service system in Tanganyika's colonial government. Trained to be a teacher, he instead became a politician, convinced that he could do more for his native land by "waging a war" against colonialism than by continuing to teach. In 1953 he was elected leader of the Tanganyika African Association, later the TANU political party. His platform was *uhuru na umoja,* or "freedom and unity," later the motto of independent Tanzania. In 1956 and again in 1957 he went before the United Nations to plead for Tanganyikan independence. His pleas were heard. It soon became obvious that Britain could no longer hold back the strong tide of nationalism that had developed in Tanganyika.

In 1961, independence finally came to Tanganyika; it came peacefully, with no conflict or struggle. Julius Nyerere became the country's first prime minister. In

Below: Julius Nyerere is sworn in as independent Tanganyika's first Prime Minister.

1962 he resigned from this post to be elected the first president of Tanganyika. Now the people usually refer to him as *Mwalimu,* which in Swahili means "teacher." They say he is teaching them how to be good nation builders.

INDEPENDENT ZANZIBAR

People on Zanzibar were also concerned about their voice in the government. There was deep resentment at the fact that an Arab sultan, under British protection, governed all the people of the islands. By 1957 an African political party called the Afro-Shirazi had been organized on Zanzibar. This party represented those Africans who felt they were not always treated fairly by their Arab rulers.

Zanzibar did not have as easy a time in its fight for independence as did Tanganyika. Arabs had ruled harshly and without African consent for hundreds of years. Many Africans still felt hostile to the Arabs. The British protectorate did little

Left: Julius Nyerere resigned as Prime Minister to become the first president of Tanganyika. A month later, in December, 1962, Tanganyika became a republic (opposite).

TANGANYIKA NEWS REVIEW

TANGANYIKA
NEWS REVIEW

PUBLISHED BY TANGANYIKA INFORMATION SERVICES, DAR ES SALAAM.   DECEMBER 1962

SALUTE TO A NEW REPUBLIC

The time was a minute past midnight. The date, December 9. Tanganyika had just become a Republic within the Commonwealth and fireworks were bursting high above the heads of 75,000 cheering people in the National Stadium, Dar es Salaam. Throughout the country, the people rejoiced.

Ilikuwa usiku wa manane tarehe 9 Desemba. Ndio kwanza Tanganyika iwe Jamuhuri katika Jumuiya ya Madola, wakati myali ya fataki za moto ilipoangaza juu ya umati wa watu wasiopungua 75,000 waliokuwa wakishangilia kwenye Uwanja wa Taifa, Dar es Salaam. Watu walisheheka kila mahala katika nchi.

to alter the bad feelings between the Arabs and the Africans of Zanzibar.

The Afro-Shirazi political party was the African voice in the politics of Zanzibar. It campaigned hard, but when independence finally came to Zanzibar in 1963, the Arab faction won control of the new government. The Afro-Shirazi party did not believe the election results reflected the true wishes of the people, because the British had apportioned electoral districts so the Arab minority could retain control. The Arab minority government, however, lasted barely a month after independence was granted in December 1963. On January 12, 1964, a revolution occurred and the Afro-Shirazi party took control of the government of Zanzibar.

UNITY AND UJAMAA

By April of 1964, the leaders of Zanzibar and Tanganyika had agreed to join together to form one independent nation. Tanzania was selected for the nation's new name—*tan* for Tanganyika and *zan* for Zanzibar. The union of these two nations into one independent republic is celebrated each year on April 26—Union Day.

Tanzania's President Nyerere and his government have created a plan called *ujamaa*, or African Socialism, for developing the economy of the country. The word *ujamaa* is a Swahili word meaning "familyhood," the traditional extended family way of life well known to most Africans. It is a way of living and working together so that everyone helps one another. President Nyerere first announced this plan in February of 1967. In what was called the Arusha Declaration, Nyerere said that the government would dedicate itself to implementing *ujamaa* as a way of developing the nation.

There were three important characteristics in traditional *ujamaa* living: every member of the family was respected; all members of the group were obligated to work; and everything was owned and shared by all members of the group. All members did not share equally, but no one received more than another until after everyone had his basic needs. Extras then were given to those who had performed additional services.

Under the Arusha Declaration, *ujamaa* was expanded and tailored to the needs of a whole nation instead of a small family group. All people were to respect one another. No one would be allowed to suffer from hunger, lack of proper housing, or lack of adequate clothing, because all goods would be shared. Everyone would have at least his basic needs. Important items would be commonly owned, or "owned" by the government.

The major industries of Tanzania were *nationalized*, taken over by the government, at the time of the Arusha Declaration. A plan was worked out so that the original owners of these industries would be paid. This program of nationalization insured that qualified Tanzanians would be able to get jobs. Those who contributed extra work could accumulate extra goods and benefits. In following these principles, everyone would be working together to help support the nation.

President Nyerere was afraid that a privileged class of rich officials might develop that would be out of touch with the common people. Thus, he cut his own salary and asked his leading government officials to cut theirs, too—which they did.

The entire development of Tanzania was to be based on this tradition. *Ujamaa* has become more than a word to the people of Tanzania. It is a way of life.

Everyone works together to build a new ujamaa *village at Mwese Tabora.*

TANZANIA
PROVINCES

Bukoba
Musoma
MARA
WEST LAKE
MWANZA
Mwanza
Arusha
Moshi
SHINYANGA
Shinyanga
ARUSHA
KILIMANJARO
Kigoma
Singida
Tanga
Wete
PEMBA
KIGOMA
Tabora
TANGA
Singida
DODOMA
TABORA
SINGIDA
ZANZIBAR
Dodoma
Zanzibar
Morogoro
COAST
Dar es Salaam
MBEYA
Iringa
MOROGORO
IRINGA
Mbeya
MTWARA
Songea
Mtwara
RUVUMA

TANZANIA AND THE WORLD

The people of Tanzania have tried to maintain an open policy of friendship with the important nations of the world. President Nyerere said, "We wish to be friendly with all, and we will never allow our friends to choose our enemies for us." With these goals in mind, it is not surprising that Tanzania is an active member of the United Nations. The government has also been a powerful contributing member of the Organization of African Unity. Most of the independent nations of Africa are members of this group.

Tanzania has also been extremely sympathetic to people living in areas that still suffer racial discrimination or are under colonial rule. For these reasons, Tanzania does not maintain relations with the white minority governments of South Africa and Rhodesia nor with the nation of Portugal, which still maintains several colonies in Africa.

After the three East African nations—Tanzania, Kenya, and Uganda—had achieved independence, they formed a group called the East African Community. This group enables these three closely related nations to work together on such matters as trade and transportation. The Community works together to maintain East African Railways, a post and telegraph system, and East African Airways, and to set common tariffs (taxes) on imports and exports to other nations. At times this cooperative effort has been difficult to maintain, but Tanzania has tried as much as possible to work with other nations for the benefit of all.

THE GOVERNMENT

Tanzania's official name is the United Republic of Tanzania. Its government is a democracy, but the two areas of the country are each controlled by a separate political party—the TANU party on the mainland and the Afro-Shirazi party in Zanzibar. Each party determines how the government's policies will be put into effect in its area.

The president is the major executive officer of the government. He is assisted by two vice-presidents. The first vice-president is concerned exclusively with Zanzibar. The second vice-president takes care of problems that relate only to mainland Tanzania.

The legislative branch of the government is called the National Assembly. Composed of elected representatives from all over the country, it assists the executive branch of the government. Members of the National Assembly are elected for terms of five years.

Even though Tanzania has a one-party system of democracy, usually no person is allowed to run for a political office unopposed. The political party presents two candidates for the same office. The voters then decide which one can handle the job better. The government believes that more than one political party is unnecessary, since all people have the same general goal—to build a strong independent nation.

EDUCATION

One of the most important needs of people in most new nations is education. Many colonial governments neglected the education of an area's native people. Newly independent governments realize that the people need to learn the skills necessary to build up their country. In the first five years after independence, primary school enrollment in Tanzania increased 53 percent while secondary school enrollment doubled. Despite this seemingly fantastic rate of progress, half the children of Tanzania still cannot attend school. The government hopes that by 1980, it will be able to provide schooling for all the children in the country.

Since Tanzania has a great deal of farmland, the schools encourage study of the important farming skills. In primary

Though primary school enrollment increased 53 percent during the first five years after independence, half the children of Tanzania still cannot attend school.

schools, pupils are taught basic farming skills as well as the usual academic subjects. In school garden projects, children grow different kinds of foods.

Students who continue on to secondary school often study scientific and technical subjects, which are considered very important by the government of this developing nation. After the students finish secondary school many continue their education. The Dar es Salaam Technical College offers a wide variety of technical courses for these students. Such fields as electronics, mining, automobile and truck repairing, welding, and secretarial skills are offered here. Teachers are badly needed in Tanzania, and the nation has a number of teacher training colleges.

The University of Dar es Salaam offers degrees in the arts, sciences, and law. Schools of medicine, engineering, and agriculture are being started at the university. Students who graduate from the University of Dar es Salaam often go to foreign countries to continue their studies.

These very young primary school students are learning motor skills.

TANZANIA INFORMATION SERVICES

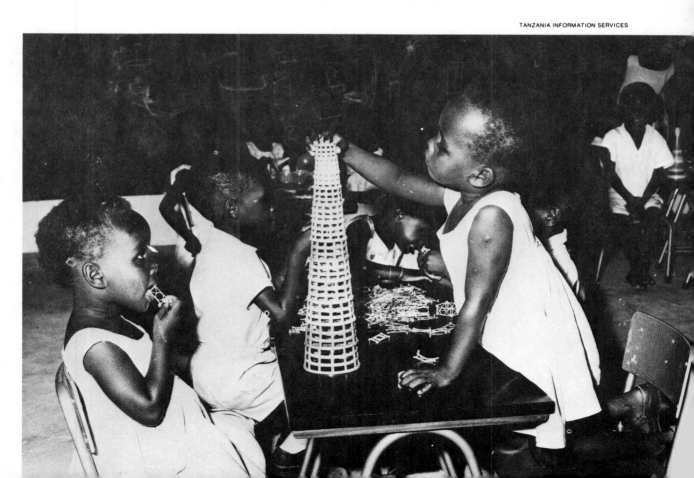

Children at a self-help school recently completed near Arusha.

Right: This charming girl is studying in a primary school in Kigoma.
Below: Education for self-reliance is taught in Tanzanian schools. These people are learning how to handle sisal after it has been brought in from the fields.

TANZANIA INFORMATION SERVICES

The men and women pictured on this page are attending adult education classes at Shinyanga. Hundreds of thousands of adults who have never learned to read and write now have the opportunity to learn.

TANZANIA INFORMATION SERVICES

MICHAEL ROBERTS

Above and below: Very modern campus of the University of Dar es Salaam.

Below: Kivukoni College, Dar es Salaam, is run by the Tanganyika Education Trust Fund.

LUFTHANSA-ARCHIV

Natural Treasures

MINERAL TREASURES

Only about half of mainland Tanzania has been geographically mapped. There is no official listing of the kinds of minerals found in the rest of the country, or where they are located. So far, most of the known mineral deposits are located near the borders of the country. The United Nations has sent mineralogists (mineral experts) to study the uncharted areas. The Mineral Resources Division of the Tanzanian government has also organized geological surveys to locate and develop new resources.

After the minerals are discovered, however, there is a problem in getting the minerals out. This is mostly because the minerals are in remote regions and there is not enough money to build transport lines. This situation is improving, though, especially with the construction of the TanZam railroad that will pass through some of Tanzania's mineral-rich areas.

One important recent mineral discovery has been a very beautiful stone that could be used in making jewelry. It has been named tanzanite and is mostly found near Arusha. The government wants to be sure

Completion of the TanZam railroad, which will pass through mineral rich areas, will help in the transportation of minerals from remote areas.

TANZANIA INFORMATION SERVICES

57

it receives proper payment for the tanzanite it exports, but so many people are interested in it that smuggling has become a problem.

Diamonds that are used for jewelry have been mined for many years, mostly near Lake Victoria. They make up the principal exported mineral, and are mined from open pits rather than underground mines.

Another important mineral source is the remote Lake Nyasa region, where coal and iron ore were discovered in the 1920s. The TanZam railway, connecting the Copperbelt in Zambia with the ocean port of Dar es Salaam, will pass near this region, making it possible to mine and ship these minerals to foreign countries and to other parts of Tanzania.

Other minerals found in the country include gold, copper, oil, natural gas, tin, and lead. Most of the known gold deposits were exhausted many years ago, but UN mineralogists think there might be more gold near Lake Victoria or in the south near Zambia and Malawi. Romania is helping Tanzania search for copper in the Kigugwe area, east of the city of Mbeya. Along the coastline and under the Zanzibar Channel, a search is under way for oil and natural gas. Tin is found in small deposits near Rwanda and Uganda, and there is some lead near Lake Tanganyika.

LIVING THINGS

Cattle raising has long been important, mostly in the central plateau region. Until recently, the cattle were raised more as a symbol of wealth than as a source of meat. For hundreds of years, the Masai people have raised cattle throughout East Africa. The Masai believe that God gave cattle only to them and that no one else is supposed to have any. But the Masai do not

The Masai keep cattle as a symbol of wealth, though the government is trying to convince them to raise cattle for food. This Masai woman feeds the small family herd.

TANZANIA INFORMATION SERVICES

eat the cattle, though they use the milk. Instead, they just keep it. The more cattle a person owns, the more status he has.

Today the government is trying to convince the Masai that they should live on cattle ranches and raise their cattle for food. It is very difficult, however, to tell a people who roam over thousands of square miles each year that they now must stay within a few hundred acres. Many of their cattle are ill with such diseases as tuberculosis and the Masai themselves are undernourished. The government is making great efforts to treat these problems.

There are many wild animals in Tanzania, found mostly in zoos or game parks. These include elephants, lions, antelope, zebras, and buffalo. Because the government is afraid these valuable animals will be destroyed by hunters, game reserves have been set up to provide permanent homes for them. People are taught how to work with the animals at the College of African Wildlife Management in Mweka.

TANZANIA INFORMATION SERVICES

Left: This waterpoint for cattle was built at Monduli, Masailand through self-help. Below: This elephant herd was encountered by a group of students and instructors from the college of African Wildlife Management. Training at the college includes the stalking of wild animals in the bush to learn about their habits and environment.

UNITED NATIONS

Tanzanians from three groups. Above: A Masai woman. Right: A Chagga chief. Below: Three Makonde women, two wearing lip plugs.

The People Live in Tanzania

MANY DIFFERENCES

There are approximately twelve million people living in Tanzania. The majority are black African people. The remainder of the population is made up of about one hundred thousand Asians and about twenty thousand Europeans.

Within the African population are about one hundred different groups, most of whom speak a language from the Bantu family of languages. It is believed that these people began to migrate gradually into the region about two thousand years ago.

In Tanzania, the principal group of Bantu-speakers is the Sukuma, numbering over a million members. Other groups are the Nwamwezi, Ha, Makonde, Gogo, Haya, Chagga, and the Hehe. The Masai, a Nilotic-speaking group that originated in the area of the Nile River, also live in Tanzania. With such a variety of people making up the population of this country, it is no surprise that the population speaks many languages.

Because the country could not conduct its business when everyone spoke a different language, Swahili was adopted as the national language. Swahili is a Bantu-based language with many Arabic and English influences. The English language is widely used in business and in the schools. Many Tanzanians are trilingual; they speak three languages. Their first language, the one they learn from their parents, is one of the many ethnic-group languages. Swahili is used when speaking with a person of a different ethnic group, and English is important in business.

Many of the people of Tanzania practice animism, a religion based on tribal traditions. Animists believe that everything—human beings, animals, material objects—has a spirit within that must be respected. The spirits of dead ancestors must be worshiped. Spirit forces control the stars, rain, wind, and other natural elements.

Islam, the religion brought to Africa by Arabs, has a large following in Tanzania. There are about three million Moslems among the African people of Tanzania. The Christian faiths also are well represented, with about 2.5 million followers.

Many of Tanzania's Asian residents practice the Hindu religion.

The Asians are having many non-religious problems. The independent East African governments have passed laws that prohibit noncitizens from maintaining businesses and holding jobs within each country. As long as a person is a citizen, his race is not important, though most Tanzanian citizens are black Africans. These laws have placed the noncitizen Asian population in a precarious position, for the Asians who kept their British citizenship after independence are now being made to leave East Africa. Under Great Britain's quota system, only a few people can move there each year. India,

Pakistan, and Bangladesh, the homelands of most of Tanzania's Asians, are already overpopulated and do not want any more people. Thus, the status of the Asian noncitizen in Tanzania is a questionable issue.

FASHION

Today very few people wear traditional dress in the cities and towns of Tanzania. Instead, they have adopted European and American fashions and added a few uniquely African touches. In the cities Tanzanian men wear pants and simple, collarless shirts. Modestly styled Western dresses with colorful head ties are worn by the women. Arab and Asian influences can also be found in the dress of native Tanzanians. Most of the Asians continue to wear the kind of clothing worn in their native land. An Indian woman can always be identified by the beautiful *sari* she wears. A sari is a six-foot long piece of fabric wrapped around the body from shoulder to ankles and pinned at the shoulder. In the rural areas local women wear *kanga* wraparounds. These are two rather brightly colored cloths, each

Women in traditional kanga *wraparounds on their way to market.*

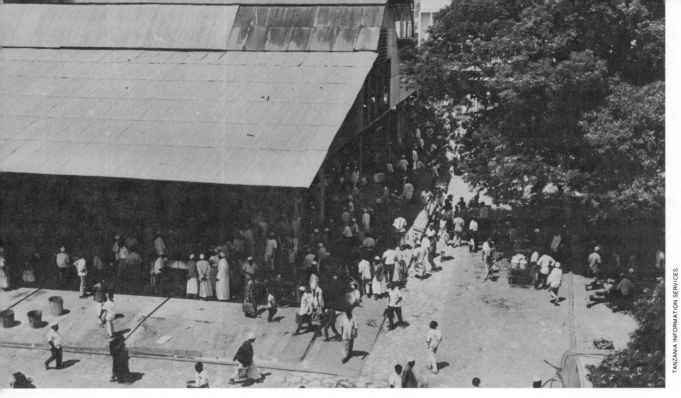

The many foods available to Tanzanians are sold in both rural and city markets. Above: The huge covered market in Dar es Salaam. Below: A typical rural outdoor market.

measuring about one yard by two yards. One is twisted around the body, the other draped over head and shoulders.

The diet of the people of Tanzania is varied because there are many available foods. Cassava (a plant with edible roots), maize, plantain (a bananalike plant), millet, and rice form the basic staple foods of the people. Vegetables such as tomatoes, cabbages, onions, and peppers, and spices such as the cloves and cinnamon that are produced on Zanzibar, are sold in markets. These vegetables and spices are added to the staple foods to make the dishes tastier. A variety of meats and fish are also available in Tanzania, and mangoes, oranges, bananas, lemons, papaw (a melonlike fruit), and pineapple are only a few of the fresh fruits that grow in abundance. Because nonnative Tanzanians brought their own foods to the country, today many Chinese dishes, as well as Indian curries and British steak and kidney pies, are popular throughout the land.

Below: Though in most countries women act as merchants in the marketplace, in Tanzania the men perform that chore.

THE ARTS

The making of artifacts has long been important in East Africa. Tanzanian museums contain many excellent examples of the artifacts of the nation's people. Many kinds of headdresses, masks, drums, musical instruments, and sculptures can be seen. Sculpture by the Makonde people is extremely popular today. Many of their newer pieces may be seen on display in shops throughout East Africa.

The people of Zanzibar were noted for hand-carved wooden archways and doors. Handsome works of these Zanzibar craftsmen are priceless reminders of the island's cultural past and today are maintained by the government in their natural settings. Their exportation is restricted by law.

Music and stories that originated centuries ago have been passed down orally from generation to generation. Until recently, none of them were ever written down. This is because most of the African

Below: Makonde wood sculptors at work.
Opposite: Some examples of their very popular sculptures.

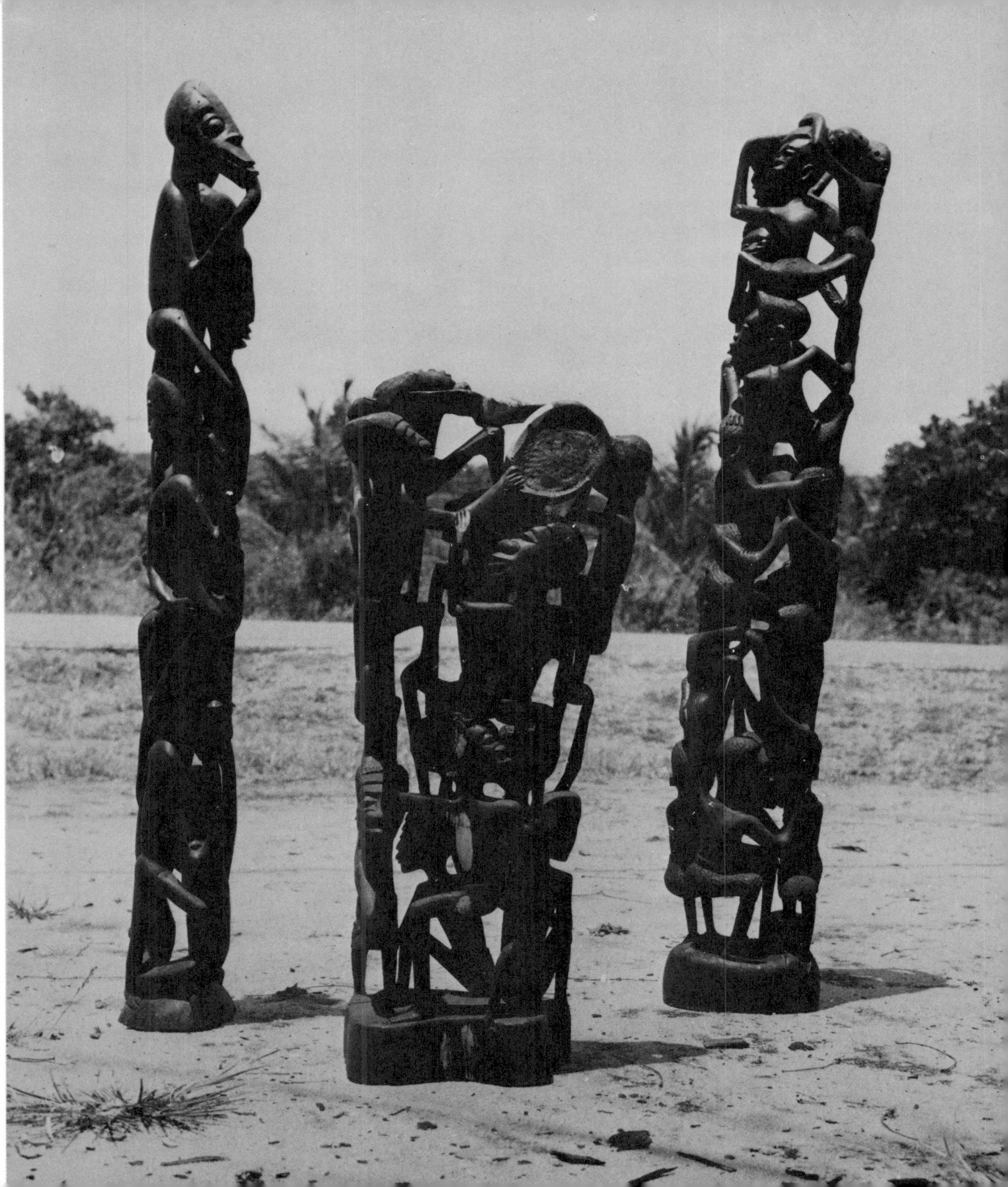

TANZANIA INFORMATION SERVICES

Above: Women getting water for their families in the traditional way—by hauling it from the rivers. Below: Waterpoints like this one, built through self-help at Ndungu, are helping to modernize the country's water systems.

languages except for Swahili, which is written in an Arabic script, were spoken rather than written languages. In recent times, many books and recordings have been made to preserve some of these early tales and songs for future generations.

Contemporary writings have not been neglected. The East Africa Literature Bureau and the East African Publishing House have encouraged their development. Recently many excellent novels, dramas, poems, and short story collections have been published as a result of efforts by these agencies to encourage African authors to continue working.

SOCIAL PROBLEMS

Tanzania's major areas of concern are disease, poverty, and illiteracy (the inability to read and write).

In addition to the more common diseases faced by people throughout the world today, Tanzanians have to cope with malaria, malnutrition, sleeping sickness, schistosomiasis (a disease of the blood and tissues caused by parasitic flatworms), smallpox, polio, and measles. These diseases have kept down the life expectancy of the average Tanzanian to about thirty-five or forty years, as compared to the sixty-five or seventy years in the more developed regions of the world. One major goal of the Tanzanian government is to increase the life expectancy to age fifty by 1980. National hospitals and health centers, voluntary missions from foreign countries, and private and industrial medical care centers have been established to provide health care.

Malaria is a particularly prevalent disease in the hot climates of Zanzibar and Pemba. The Malaria Control Project on these islands has reduced the threat of malaria a great deal since the project was undertaken. The United Nations International Children's Emergency Fund (UNICEF), the World Health Organization (WHO), and the UN Food and Agricultural Organization (FAO) have also been making great headway in solving some of Tanzania's nutrition and health problems.

In order to reduce poverty and illiteracy, the government established the Ministry of Local and Rural Development. This agency sends trained staff members to towns and villages to assist the people in a variety of projects. Some community groups build schools, dispensaries, and clinics; some teach new farm methods; and others develop and improve sanitation facilities.

A number of ministry staff people have been trained to work with the hundreds of thousands of adults who have never learned how to read and write. During the first five years after independence, more than seven hundred thousand people who never went to school had the opportunity to learn these skills. Even now, though, about 80 or 90 percent of the adult population remains illiterate.

Besides programs designed to teach people how to read and write, there are also those that teach child care, nutrition, sewing, household skills, poultry keeping, and gardening. Pregnant women attend classes to learn how to take care of themselves before their babies are born. In the more remote regions, many programs are conducted over the radio, since there is at least one radio in every village. Many instructors bring traveling teaching units from village to village. These teachers use films, posters, and other visual aids to help explain needed skills.

The government encourages its educated people to do things well and to serve as models for others by working with them.

Even President Nyerere makes it a common practice to spend a certain amount of time working the land. He wants to encourage belief in the dignity of hard work while also showing that it is necessary for everyone to share in work so all may share in the benefits.

HOUSING

Most of the people of Tanzania live in rural areas where houses have been built without the benefit of proper water and sanitation facilities. Under the government's new rural development programs,

On these pages: Most rural housing in Tanzania has been built without the benefit of proper water and sanitation facilities. The government is now helping the people build new houses with up-to-date facilities.

people can build new houses from local materials. Government workers teach the people why clean water and adequate sanitation are necessary. These people are then given help in constructing up-to-date water and sanitation systems.

In urban areas, housing projects are being constructed for people with low incomes. The government makes land sites available, constructs the basic foundations, and makes the remaining building materials available to the people. The residents must complete the remainder of the house through cooperative self-help projects. Efforts such as these have helped to increase the number of homes available in a short period of time.

A UNITED COUNTRY

The government of Tanzania wants its citizens to think of themselves as Tanzanians first and members of a particular ethnic group second. The government, however, is aware that much cultural heritage may be lost in the rapid period of development following independence. For that reason, the Ministry of Local and Rural Development is also responsible for preserving and encouraging African culture, and for developing Swahili as a national language. This ministry has done a great deal in the villages to encourage traditional dancing, music, drama, handicrafts, and games.

The Tanzanian government's Ministry of Local and Rural Development is encouraging the preservation of African culture, including traditional dancing. Opposite: Masai dancers performing. Below: Young traditional snake dancers.

The People Work in Tanzania

In an address to the nation, President Julius Nyerere said: "Development brings freedom, provided it is development of people. But people cannot be developed; they can only develop themselves." The government has created five-year plans to help guide this development. The first five-year plan was put into effect after the formation of the republic in 1964; it made many great advances. Now the second plan hopes to go forward even further under the spirit of *ujamaa. Ujamaa*-inspired cooperative efforts in agriculture and industry are encouraged so there will be no great differences in the accumulation of income and wealth among the people.

AGRICULTURE

Tanzania is not particularly blessed with rich land, and not enough of the land has been properly used. Too often, individual families owned small plots of land on which they tried to grow a variety of crops for their own use. It was too expensive and difficult for one family to buy and use modern machinery or to develop irrigation systems that would insure the best crop production. Now, under *ujamaa,* neighboring farmers work together on large tracts of land. The government helps by providing modern machines and instruction in new farming methods.

Opposite: Under ujamaa, *neighboring farmers work together on large tracts of land. This system improves crop productivity and improves the group's standard of living.*

Ujamaa *workers cleaning cotton.*

Cooperative villages called *ujamaa vijijini* have been set up by the government to make cooperative work easier. If these farmers can increase production in a wide variety of crops, health problems such as malnutrition will be solved. The people in these cooperative villages work together to improve their productivity, and then everyone shares in the returns. More crops will be needed not only in the rural regions, but for the growing city populations as well. Hopefully, more food products will be exported to other parts of the world.

At present, agriculture provides about 50 percent of Tanzania's income. Tanzania's most important crops are cotton, coffee, sisal, tea, and pyrethrum. Most of the cotton is grown near Lake Victoria, but some comes from the coastal strip and from the area around Kilosa, west of Dar

es Salaam. If the coastal strip were extensively irrigated, it would produce very fine cotton.

Because coffee needs a cooler climate than cotton, much of it is grown in the hilly regions of mainland Tanzania. There are enormous coffee plantations near Mt. Kilimanjaro, on the border with Kenya, and also near Rwanda and Uganda.

Sisal, which is grown along the coast, is a plant whose fiber is used to make strong ropes. For years it was a very important crop. Recently, however, synthetic products have been used more often for this purpose, since they are cheaper and last longer. This poses a problem to Tanzania because the country must earn money through its few export crops.

Tea is also an important crop. Because it requires a warm to cool climate, with a substantial amount of rain, it is grown in

Tea is an important crop grown in the highlands. The tea factory at left is in the Usumbora Mountains in the Tanga region.
Below: Coffee, another important crop, is grown mainly on the slopes of Mount Kilimanjaro. Here Chagga women sort coffee beans in the sun outside their typical Chagga home.

Sisal, a plant whose fiber is used to make strong rope, used to be a very important crop for Tanzania. Though synthetic products are now being used more often for this purpose, sisal is still grown along the coast of Tanzania. On these pages are shown some of the steps in sisal production. Left: Cut sisal from fields (below) being carried to nearby factory. Opposite top: Sisal fibers drying at factory. Opposite bottom: Dry sisal fibers inside the factory.

Fishing has long been an important occupation in Tanzania. On this page: Traditional fishermen with their coconut tree canoes on Lake Kitangira Singida.

the highlands. In the southwest near Lake Malawi are vast farms that produce tea.

More cloves are produced in Zanzibar than in any other part of the world. Because cloves are so important to Zanzibar, they are the major symbol of the island group. Once they are planted, cloves grow almost without care or attention.

Although there is still a market for these cash crops, the world market has steadily declined. Sisal is being replaced by synthetic fibers. Pyrethrum (a flower whose leaves are used to make insecticides) is being threatened by chemicals that can produce insecticides of better quality for less cost than the pyrethrum leaves. Because there has been increased production of coffee in other developing nations of the world, the demand for coffee is less than the supply. The Tanzanian government is concerned with these factors, and is trying to find new crops for Tanzanian farmers. Plans are in progress to produce cotton, tea, tobacco, and wheat in large-scale operations similar to plantations. Efforts are also being made to increase production of such crops as corn and rice, along with assorted vegetables and fruits. There is great demand for more millet, sugar, and bananas.

Fishing has long been important on both the mainland and on Zanzibar, since there is so much coastline. In recent years, the government has been trying to expand the fishing industry on the mainland. The seacoast areas provide an abundance of marlin, sailfish, tuna, barracuda, and kingfish. Many interior mountain streams have excellent trout and bass. Factories that process, can, and store fish are being built as fast as they are needed.

Tanzania also has large forests of such hardwoods as teak, ebony, and camphorwood. Some of this wood is used within the country, and some is sold to other nations.

These fishermen are on an inlet at Bukoba on the shores of Lake Victoria.

BUSINESS

In colonial and protectorate times, Tanzania primarily exported raw materials and imported manufactured products. When Tanzania became an independent republic, it had to develop its own industries. President Nyerere's Arusha Declaration of 1967 announced that the government would take control of most of the industries within the nation. This means that Tanzania is under *socialism,* a system in which the government controls the major industries, farms, and other means of production.

At the time of the Arusha Declaration, however, Tanzania had very few industries. There were four mills where sisal fiber was spun into rope, three textile mills, and an oil refinery at Dar es Salaam. Shortly after the Arusha Declaration, a cement factory, a radio assembly plant, a cashew nut processing plant, some soap factories, and several shoe factories were built. In time, other industries were added—plants that assemble trucks and farm equipment and plants that produce bicycle tires, beverages, tobacco, pharmaceuticals, insecticides, and aluminum foil.

The second five-year plan includes a project to bring electricity to more remote parts of the country. Three new plants to manufacture electricity are planned. These will meet the country's needs for at least a few years.

Diamond mining is an important industry in Tanzania, and most of the diamonds are exported, bringing in a great amount of foreign money. Unfortunately, however, Tanzania does not have a favorable balance of trade; the country must import far more than it exports. Because industrial development is still limited many items found in stores—as well as most machinery, cars and trucks, and fuel—must be imported.

Shortly after the Arusha Declaration, several factories were built, including this cement factory.

TANZANIA INFORMATION SERVICES

FINANCE

In most of the developing nations of the world, there is a great fear that money earned within the country's borders will be taken out of the country and spent elsewhere, rather than invested in business and developments within the country. If money goes out and is not put back into the economy, a nation can soon become bankrupt. (This can happen to well-established nations, too.) Tanzania is greatly concerned about this problem.

The Bank of Tanzania controls all the major banking functions in the country. It issues currency and controls the international exchange of Tanzania's money. The Bank of Tanzania works with foreign companies that are considering investing in Tanzania. It also gives loans and other incentives to Tanzanians who want to build large industrial or residential projects. As Tanzania's economy becomes more stable, the strict laws about money will probably become looser.

TRANSPORTATION

One of the most ambitious transportation projects in Africa is the TanZam Railway. Aided by the People's Republic of China, the governments of Tanzania and Zambia constructed approximately eleven hundred miles of railroad, linking the seaport city of Dar es Salaam in Tanzania to the rich copper mines of north-central Zambia. This project costs approximately the equivalent of 400 million U.S. dollars. Both countries will benefit from this railroad. Landlocked Zambia will have an outlet to the sea for her valuable copper, and Tanzania's interior will develop faster as products move back and forth along the railroad.

This is not the first railroad in Tanzania. For many years East African Rail-

Rails being fixed in concrete sleepers at one of the workshops of the TanZam railway line. Construction of this railway line is one of the most ambitious projects in Africa.

TANZANIA INFORMATION SERVICES

Kilimanjaro International Airport.

ways has been operating both passenger and freight service over some two thousand miles of railroads in Tanzania, Kenya, and Uganda.

New highways are also important to Tanzania. Many roads link various parts of the nation already, but not all of these roads can be used year-round. Heavy rainfall makes some of them impassable part of the time. Plans have been made to improve many of these roads for permanent use. A new highway system has been built to parallel the TanZam Railway, providing another link to the interior and to neighboring Zambia. Truck service over a highway to Zambia has been possible since 1966.

Tanzania has many excellent harbors. Dar es Salaam is a very important ocean port for all of East Africa. Zanzibar and Pemba have ports of their own. Ferry service maintained on Lake Victoria at the ports of Mwanza and Bukoba make travel and shipping to and from Kenya and Uganda very easy.

Air transportation within Tanzania is very important. East African Airlines, cooperatively maintained by Tanzania, Uganda, and Kenya, not only flies within East Africa but also provides access to all parts of the world. The airline has a modern fleet of airplanes, maintained and staffed by East African personnel. This is quite an achievement for a developing region. The Dar es Salaam International Airport is host to numerous airlines from all corners of the world.

Postal and telegraph services within East Africa are handled by the Cooperative Common Services Authority. Mail within Tanzania is carried by road, rail, and air.

New highways are being built in Tanzania to improve transportation routes in the country. One new highway system parallels the TanZam Railway, providing another link to the interior and to neighboring Zambia.

TANZANIA INFORMATION SERVICES

Enchantment of Tanzania

ENCHANTMENT OF TANZANIA

Home of the proud Masai people, home of one of the greatest varieties of animal life anywhere, and home of a people working together in *ujamaa* to build up their country—all this makes up part of the enchantment of Tanzania. This nation, divided into two parts by the Zanzibar Channel, contains much of the history, beauty, and mystery that represents the African continent in the minds of many people today.

GAME PARKS

Mainland Tanzania's national parks and animal reserves have perhaps the world's finest concentration of game. There are seven national parks established in the country. No one is allowed to live in these parks except the animals and here they are protected from human harm. Game reserves have also been established, where hunting is permitted only under government supervision. Only certain species of animals may be hunted, and only at certain times of the year. Usually these are species that are in danger of becoming overpopulous. Revenue from park fees and hunting permits is used to aid in wildlife conservation and preservation efforts throughout Tanzania.

Serengeti National Park is one of the most spectacular of all the national parks. More than one million animals make Serengeti their home. The animals live in total freedom on plains covering approximately five thousand square miles of land. Counts made by park rangers estimate the lion population to be about two

Lake Manyara Park lion resting in the limbs of a large acacia tree.

thousand strong, the wildebeest over three hundred thousand, and the zebra herd at almost two hundred thousand. Besides these animals the park has more than thirty-five other species of plains animals. Many birds also live in this park.

One fact that makes Serengeti National Park so different from any other park in Africa is the "Serengeti migration" that occurs each year in late May or June. From December to early May, most of the wildlife graze in the southern portion of the park. Then, as the water supplies decrease during the dry season, wildebeests and zebras migrate by the thousands to the northern regions of the park where permanent watering holes are available. This seeming flood of animals crossing the Serengeti Plains is an unforgettable sight.

Many excellent tourist accommodations are available throughout the park. There is a variety of comfortable sleeping and eating facilities.

Lake Manyara National Park is another magnificent park in Tanzania. It is located in the great Rift Valley; on one side of this park is the steep wall of the Rift Valley escarpment (cliffs). This wall rises about a thousand feet straight up, and atop this wall a resort hotel overlooks the vast water and forest area of the park. In this setting are such animals as lions, elephants, rhinoceroses, impalas, giraffes, leopards, zebras, waterbucks, and different varieties of monkeys.

The lions of Lake Manyara Park are extremely popular subjects for photographers. These lions have developed the habit of resting in the limbs of large acacia trees some ten to twenty feet above the ground during the heat of the day. Cars can drive underneath one of these

Ngorongoro Crater is home of both animals and people. The cheetahs at left share their domain with rhinoceroses (below) and zebras (bottom), as well as with Masai herdsmen and their cattle.

branches and the passengers can gaze up at the sleeping lions, sprawled and dangling in the tree limbs above.

Lake Manyara is also noted for its bird life. More than 350 species have been officially recorded here. The great number of pink flamingos that live along the border of the lake create the illusion of a vast pink ring around this body of water.

Ngorongoro Crater is a slightly different type of game sanctuary. Both animals and people live here. More than three thousand square miles of countryside were set aside for the protection of wildlife, but Masai herdsmen who had always lived in the park area would not leave, so they have been permitted to live and herd their cattle there. Park visitors viewing a pride of lions from within the protective setting of a closed-up minibus are often shocked to see a group of Masai herders and their cattle walking unconcerned near the wild animals.

HAVEN OF PEACE

One of the most charming capital cities in Africa is Tanzania's Dar es Salaam. This city received its name hundreds of years ago from the early Arab explorers who thought of this beautiful ocean port as a *dar es salaam,* or "haven of peace."

Tall coconut palm trees line the harbor area where ships from all over the world anchor. Sandy beach areas north and south of the harbor await swimmers and sun worshipers. These white and silver sandy beaches extend for many miles along the coastal strip. The blue-green warm water of the Indian Ocean is a most delightful attraction. Many resort hotels are available for the crowds that come to the Tanzanian coast from all over the world.

Away from the oceanside is the National Museum at Dar es Salaam. Here can be seen the original skull bones of *Zinjanthropus,* found by Dr. L.S.B. Leakey at the Olduvai Gorge. About two million years old, the *Zinjanthropus* is a relative of early man. The Village Museum nearby contains many examples of traditional housing and artifacts used by the various groups of people in the country. Local artisans often work on their crafts at the museum, and interested visitors often watch these skilled artists at work.

HIGH POINT OF AFRICA

Perhaps the most impressive sight in all of Tanzania is Mount Kilimanjaro, the highest point in Africa.

According to early legends, this mountain was believed to be a throne for God, who had created this earth. People believed that when God wished to come to earth, he would sit upon his mountain throne and rest while he watched his land and people below. It was also believed that heavenly warriors guarded the mountaintop throne. Many ancient peoples refused to climb this mountain because of their respect for God's property. Others feared the "heavenly guards," whose silver shields reflected bright sunlight from the top of the mountain. The bright reflection was probably caused by the snow and ice which is always covering the top of Mount Kilimanjaro.

In more recent times, Mount Kilimanjaro has become a popular mountain to climb, and is not a difficult trip. Hikers usually take about three days to reach the summit and two days to return. Because climbing up the peak is very strenuous at such high altitudes, it takes more time than the descent. Several comfortable hotels are situated near the base of the mountain, and they provide a relaxing point of departure for those people who wish to climb to the "top of the African continent."

ZANZIBAR

This island group is one of the most picturesque areas in all of East Africa. The contrasts of the old and new in fashion, architecture, and customs make the islands of Zanzibar and Pemba fascinating spots to visit. Many historical sites still exist on Zanzibar, such as the former sultan's palace, the old *dhow* harbor (a *dhow* is a boat used by early Arab traders), and the home used by Dr. David Livingstone during his many stays on the island. The Cathedral Church of Christ sits on the site of the old slave market. The famous "Zanzibar doors" made of teak and brass, in the area of the old city, are very beautiful.

Since the outside world learned that Tanzania existed, people have been interested in the area. Early Arabs echoed their praises of Tanzania in their writings. Nineteenth-century European explorers, such as Livingstone, Burton, and Speke, also had much to say about this area. The people of the United Republic of Tanzania are proud of their new developing nation. They are proving by their daily efforts that their new nation can develop into a strong, important member of the world community. As President Nyerere has said, "Development of the people can only be effected by the people."

The beautiful ocean port of Dar es Salaam is one of the most charming capital cities in Africa.

Handy Reference Section

INSTANT FACTS

Political:
Official name—The United Republic of Tanzania
Form of Government—republic
Monetary unit—Tanzanian shilling
Official Language—Swahili; English is widely used
Independence Day—Union Day, April 26
Flag—Three diagonal stripes of colors, separated by two thin diagonal stripes of yellow. The upper left stripe is green, which represents the land. The middle band of black stands for the people. The lower right blue stripe represents the ocean.
National Motto—*Uhuru Na Umoja* (Swahili for "Freedom and Unity")

National Shield—A man and woman holding an ivory tusk in each hand as well as supporting a shield. The shield's decorations include the torch of freedom, the national flag, and symbols of the ocean and crossed swords with a spear imposed over it all.
National Anthem—*Mungu Ibariki Afrika*

Geographical:
Area—363,708 square miles
Greatest length—740 miles
Greatest width—760 miles
Highest point—Mount Kilimanjaro, 19,340 feet
Lowest point—2,000 feet below sea level (bottom point of Lake Tanganyika)

POPULATION

National Population—12,313,469
Population Density—35 per square mile
Population Growth Rate—2.6 percent
Birth Rate—47 per 1,000
Death Rate—22 per 1,000
Average Life Span—40-41 years

Literacy Rate—85-90 percent illiterate
Principal Cities:

Dar es Salaam	275,000
Zanzibar	70,000
Tanga	60,000
Mwanza	34,000

900—Arabs trade along East African coast

1331—Ibn Battuta, Arab explorer, visits Kilwa

1502—Vasco de Gama and Portuguese ships off Tanzanian coast

1840—Zanzibar sultanate established

1871—Stanley greets Dr. Livingstone at Ujiji

1884—Berlin Conference held; Germany claims Tanganyika

1898—Mkwana dies rather than be taken prisoner of Germans

1905—Maji Maji Rebellion

1919—Great Britain takes over colonial control of Tanganyika

1922—Tanganyika Territory African Civil Servants Association formed

1922—Birth of Julius Nyerere

1946—Tanganyika placed under United Nations trusteeship; Britain remains as administrator

1953—Nyerere becomes leader of Tanganyika African Association

1954—TANU political party formed

1956—Nyerere goes to United Nations to plead for independence

1957—Nyerere makes second trip to United Nations

1957—Afro-Shirazi Party formed on Zanzibar

1959—Zinjanthropus skull found at Olduvai Gorge

1961—Tanganyika becomes independent, December 9

1962—Nyerere resigns as prime minister and is elected first president of new Republic of Tanganyika

1963—Zanzibar becomes independent, December 10

1964—Afro-Shirazi party assumes control of Zanzibar government, January 12

1964—Union Day; Zanzibar and Tanganyika become the United Republic of Tanzania, April 26

1964—First five-year-plan

1966—Truck service to Zambia begins

1967—Arusha Declaration, February

1969—Second five-year-plan put into effect

1970—Election; incumbent government retained

1973—TanZam railroad completed

Index

African Socialism, 46
Afro-Shirazi party, 44, 46, 49
Agriculture, 17, 25, 75-81
Animals, 58, 59, 86-89
Animism, 61
Arab people, 29-31, 44, 46
Archaeology, 7, 8, 28, 29
Artifacts, 66
Arusha, 21, 57
Arusha Declaration, 46, 82
Asian population, 61, 62
Aviation, 49, 84

Bank of Tanzania, 83
Belgians, 37
Berlin conference, 1884, 37
Birds, 89
British in Tanzania, 34, 37, 40, 41, 43, 44, 62
Bukoba, 84
Burundi, 10

Cathedral Church of Christ, Zanzibar, 37, 90
Cattle, 22, 24, 58, 59
China, People's Republic of, 83

Christian religion, 62
Cinnamon, 34
Climate, 15
Clothing, 62
Cloves, 30, 34, 81
Coal, 58
Coconuts, 18
Coffee, 37, 76, 81
College of African Wildlife Management, 59
Congo, 31, 34
Congo, Democratic Republic of, 10
Cooperative farms, 17, 25, 76
Copper, 58
Copra, 18, 34
Cotton, 38, 76
Crafts, 66

Dar es Salaam, 21, 26, 40, 58, 82, 83, 84, 89
Dar es Salaam International Airport, 84
Dar es Salaam Technical College, 51
Diamonds, 58, 82
Disease, 69

East Africa Literature Bureau, 69
East African Airways, 49, 84
East African Community, 49
East African Publishing House, 69
East African Railways, 49, 83
Education, 19, 21, 26, 50, 51
Electricity, 82
Engaruka (early village), 29
Ethnic groups, 61
Exports, 49, 82

Farming, 17, 25, 75-81
Finance, 83
Fish, 81
Five-year plans, 75, 82
Food, 65
Forests, 81

Gama, Vasco da, 31
Game reserves, 86
Gas, natural, 58
Geography, 9
Germans, 37, 38, 40
Government, 49

Health, 69
Hehe people, 38
Highways, 84
Hindu religion, 62
Homo habilis (early man), 8, 28
Housing, 70
Husuni Kubwa palace, Kilwa, 29

Ibn Battuta, 29
Imports, 49, 82
Independence, Tanganyika, 43
Independence, Zanzibar, 46
Independence Day, 26
Indian Ocean, 9
Industry, 82
Iringa, 38
Iron ore, 58
Islamic religion, 18, 29, 62
Ivory, 30, 31, 34

Kenya, 8, 10, 12, 25, 28, 37, 40, 49, 84
Kigugwe area, 58
Kilimanjaro, Mount, 13, 25, 38, 76, 89, 90

Kilosa, 76
Kilwa, 29, 30, 31, 38
Kizimkazi, Zanzibar, 17

Lake Manyara National Park, 87
Lakes, 10
Languages, 21, 61, 69, 73
Lead, 58
League of Nations, 40
Leakey, Louis B., 7, 8, 29, 89
Leakey, Richard, 28
Life expectancy, 69
Literacy, 69
Livingstone, David, 34, 90

Mafia Island, 12
Maji Maji Rebellion, 38
Makerere College, Uganda, 43
Malaria, 69
Malawi, 10, 58
Malawi, Lake, 10, 13, 81
Manufacturing, 82
Manyara, Lake, 87, 89
Map of Tanzania, 11
Map of Tanzania provinces, 48
Masai people, 22, 24, 25, 31, 58, 59, 61, 89
Mbeya, 58
Minerals, 57, 58
Mkwawa (chief), 38
Money, 83
Moshi, 25
Moslems, 18, 62
Motto of Tanzania, 43

Mozambique, 10, 30
Museum, National, 89
Music, 66
Mwanza, 84
Mweka, 59

National Assembly, 49
National Museum, Dar es Salaam, 89
National parks, 86, 87
Ngorongoro Crater, 22, 25, 29, 89
Nile River, 28
Nyasa, Lake, 58
Nyerere, Julius, 41-47, 49, 70, 75

Oil, 58, 82
Olduvai Gorge, 7, 8, 28, 89
Olduvai River, 7
Organization of African Unity, 49

Pemba Island, 12, 29, 69, 84, 90
Peters, Karl, 37
Population figures, 61
Ports, 84
Portuguese, 31
Postal service, 84
Poverty, 69
Prehistoric times, 28, 29
Provinces, Map of, 48
Pyrethrum, 81

Railroads, 49, 57, 83
Rainfall, 15
Religion, 18, 29, 61, 62
Rift Valley, 10, 12, 13, 29, 87
Roads, 84
Romania, 58
Rudolf, Lake (Kenya), 28
Rufiji River, 40
Rwanda, 10, 58

Savanna, 12
Schools, 19, 21, 26, 50, 51
Seasons, 15
Serengeti National Park, 12, 86
Sisal, 37, 76, 82
Slavery, 30, 31, 34
Socialism, 82
Stanley, Henry Morton, 34
Swahili culture, 29
Swahili language, 61, 69, 73

Tabora, 21, 31
Tanganyika, 37, 38, 40, 41, 43, 44, 46
Tanganyika, Lake, 10, 13, 34, 58
Tanganyika African Association, 41, 43
Tanganyikan African National Union, 41, 43
TANU party, 41, 43, 49
TanZam Railway, 57, 58, 83
Tanzania, founding of, 46
Tanzanite, 57
Tea, 76

Telegraph service, 84
Temperatures, 15
Tin, 58
Tobacco, 37
Trade, 49, 82
Transportation, 83, 84
Trees, 81

Uganda, 10, 12, 25, 28, 37, 40, 43, 49, 58, 84
Uguja (Zanzibar), 29
Ujamaa (familyhood), 46, 75
Ujiji, 34
Union Day, 46
United Nations, 41, 43, 49, 57, 69
University of Dar es Salaam, 26, 51

Victoria, Lake, 10, 13, 28, 58, 76, 84

World War I, 40
Writings, 69

Zaïre, 10
Zambia, 10, 58, 83, 84
Zanzibar, 9, 12, 17, 29, 30, 31, 34, 37, 40, 41, 44, 46, 49, 66, 69, 81, 84, 90
Zanzibar Channel, 58
"Zanzibar doors", 66, 90
Zinjanthropus, 8, 89

About the Author: Already the author of seventy-three books published by Childrens Press, Allan Carpenter is on his way again with the forty-two book "Enchantment of Africa" series. Except for a few years spent founding, editing, and publishing a teachers' magazine, Allan has worked as a free-lance writer of books and magazine articles. During his many years in publishing, he has perfected a highly organized approach to handling large volumes of material—after extensive traveling and having collected all possible materials, he systematically reviews and organizes everything. From his apartment high in the magnificent John Hancock Building, Allan recalls: "My collection and assimilation of materials on the states and countries began before the publication of my first book when I was twenty years old." When not writing or traveling, Allan also enjoys music—he has been the principal string bass player for the Chicago Business Men's Orchestra for twenty-five years.